Guided by Wisdom

Finding Wisdom for Life in God's Word

Guided by Wisdom

Finding Wisdom for Life in God's Word

Chris Long

**Book 1
in the
Every Step Series**

ISBN 979-8-9891485-0-9 (Paperback)

ISBN 979-8-9891485-1-6 (e-book)

To Daniela and David.

May you walk with the L<small>ORD</small> all your days

To never lose your way or be led astray

Riches and pleasure will want to call you away

But with the L<small>ORD</small> you'll stay, is what I pray

Luke 18:16

[16] But Jesus called them to Him and said, "Let the little children come to Me, and do not forbid them; for of such is the kingdom of God."

Contents

Acknowledgments

My wife and best friend, Caroll. This book would not have been written if it wasn't for your courage and wisdom. Through the homeschooling of our children, you have shown me how to raise children in God's Word. You showed me it was possible for very young children to want to read the Bible and to learn deeper truths in it. You are an amazing woman.

Daniela and David, your hunger for the Word of God was the true inspiration for this book. My prayer is that is shows countless children how they can benefit from that same hunger and curiosity you have for the Kingdom of God.

And to my early readers and advisors. Thank you for being dedicated to coming alongside me on this journey. You responded to the call and refused to allow this broken and imperfect man to walk this path alone. I am forever grateful.

Introduction

God always intended for us to raise our children with His Word as part of their home life and education. He lets us know early in the Bible that we are to impress His Word onto the hearts of our children when He says, in Deuteronomy 6, verse 7:

> *7 You shall teach them diligently to your children, and shall talk of them when you sit in your house, when you walk by the way, when you lie down, and when you rise up.*

Then, lest we forget this command as we read through the history of the Hebrew people and the successes and failures of the kings, He reminds us, in Isaiah 54, verse 13:

> *13 All your children shall be taught by the Lord,*
> *And great shall be the peace of your children.*

And knowing when there is something of vital importance that we need to be told again and again throughout the generations, lest we wander astray in the distractions of our day, He repeats this to us, at the beginning and at the end of the New Testament:

Matthew 19:14-15

¹⁴ But Jesus said, "Let the little children come to Me, and do not forbid them; for of such is the kingdom of heaven."
¹⁵ And He laid His hands on them and departed from there.

3 John 1:4

⁴ I have no greater joy than to hear that my children walk in truth.

The statement made by Jesus Christ cannot be made any clearer. We are to bring our children into His presence and to share the knowledge of Him with them immediately. As John shares his joy with the first generation of believers, we must also harness the same sentiment with our own children. We need to regain the desire and the courage to raise our children in the Word of God and in His truths. Our job as parents is to guide our children in the holy and righteous ways of God.

However, it is more likely for a parent to delegate this job to the secular world first, allowing the school system and peer groups to show their kids the real world, to assimilate them so they won't stand out, to educate them on how to behave and what to believe, convinced this will be the path to greater ease, more abundance, and success in life.

Guided by Wisdom

How can we disregard the power of Isaiah 54:13, where God tells us that through Him the peace of our children will be secure? It is not through the ideas and actions of our culture that will bring peace. It is through our dedication, obedience, and love for God. Peace is not the absence of discipline. It is not the absence of direction and law. It certainly is not found in the absence of God. Is this not what our society teaches to our children? A disregard for God, an absence of truth, and a disrespect for the family.

Hope for our children, no matter the outcome of world affairs, can only be found in a real and rooted relationship with their Creator. This is the purpose of this book, to give our children the guidance, knowledge, and wisdom to live this life with God by their side and in their hearts. "Guided by Wisdom," the first book in the Every Step series, will show our children how they can use the truth of the Bible to help them make decisions in real-time situations and aid them in their character building journey.

I hope this book encourages parents everywhere to stand strong and bold in their fight to raise children of faith. Raising children with and in the Word of God impacts His kingdom and this world in ways we will neither fully know nor understand in this life.

If you think you already have failed in this endeavor, then take courage—our God is a God of redemption. Start now. Start with this book. The applicability of it to real life carries strong potential to point your kids to the Bible for the answers they may be seeking.

Psalm 119:9–10

[9] *How can a young man cleanse his way?*
By taking heed according to Your word.
[10] *With my whole heart I have sought You;*
Oh, let me not wander from Your commandments!

Wisdom in God's Word

Wisdom

Proverbs 8:35–36

35 For whoever finds me finds life,
And obtains favor from the LORD;
36 But he who sins against me wrongs his own soul;
All those who hate me love death.

Proverbs 8 in the New King James Version is titled the "Excellence of Wisdom." When we talk about wisdom in this context, we are not talking about reading books, getting smart, and earning good grades in school. Wisdom in this context means respect for God. Hating wisdom is saying we aren't buying in to respecting God, our Creator. This is how we commit wrong against our own souls and are destined for death, because separating ourselves from God is the definition of sin, and sin leads to death.

Romans 6:23

23 For the wages of sin is death, but the gift of God is eternal life in Christ Jesus, our Lord.

We find life through God and His Word, by believing in His Son, Jesus, and by accepting His free gifts of unconditional love, salvation, and eternal life with Him.

Denying God is saying we do not want or need the salvation Jesus provided for us through His death and resurrection, which means we turn down His offer to be saved from our sins and to have eternal life.

Proverbs 28:5

[5] Evil men do not understand justice,
But those who seek the Lord understand all.

When we seek wisdom through our understanding of God and the study of His Word, we are given the keys, or the potential, to understanding all things. When we seek God, receive the Holy Spirit, and submit to His guidance, understanding can come through revelation. There will be times when we just know something is good, or when something is not right.

Proverbs 28 tells us an evil man can't even understand justice. This man doesn't know what it is to be fair or why it is reasonable to be punished for wrongdoing. What he does understand is how to come out on top and not lose, no matter the cost or sacrifice required of other people. If evil men can't understand justice, then they cannot understand truth. Being void of truth and justice is not a foundation we want to build our success on. In the context of wisdom, success looks a lot different from the usual descriptions the world gives us.

Proverbs 24:3–4

[3] Through wisdom a house is built,
And by understanding it is established;

> *⁴ By knowledge the rooms are filled*
> *With all precious and pleasant riches.*

It is by wisdom, the fear of God, that our house will be built and filled with riches. And what kind of riches are they? They are found in the heart, and they are precious and pleasant. The riches of an evil man come with strife, distrust, and threats attached to them. It is God who fills our hearts with what's important; the fruits of the Spirit, which are love, joy, peace, patience, kindness, goodness, faithfulness, gentleness, and self-control (see Galatians 5:22–23).

God's Word in Action

Commit to reading God's word every day. Even if it is just a verse or two. It is not about the quantity you read. Rather it is the desire to spend time with God and developing the habit to do it.

Chris Long

Fear of the Lord

Proverbs 1:7

⁷ The fear of the LORD is the beginning of knowledge,
But fools despise wisdom and instruction.

Proverbs 9:10

¹⁰ "The fear of the LORD is the beginning of wisdom,
And the knowledge of the Holy One is understanding.

The fear of the Lord is a wonderful discovery. When we say, "fear of the Lord," we mean just that: God is to be feared. The difference between this fear and worldly fear, like the fear of dangerous men or of scary movies, is that the fear of the Lord is balanced by respect and love. When we fear God, we are not driven to run *from* Him, like we would when we are afraid of something worldly; rather, we are driven to run *to* Him. Our fear of God causes us to desire Him, to honor Him, to serve Him, and to love Him.

How is that possible? God is perfect and He knows everything. He created everything—Heaven and Earth, you and me. He is awesome and perfectly holy. God is to be feared, worshipped, and respected in every way. This is why we don't use

God's name casually or as a curse word. It is why we respectfully remove our hats when we pray. It's why we kneel to Him, raise our hands to Him, and sing to Him.

The Bible tells us God loves us, and Jesus showed us how much God loves us. When we were separated from God because of our imperfection, which is our sinful nature, Jesus gave His life so we could be reunited with God. Jesus did this even though we didn't deserve it. That is how we know He is love. Think of all the ways we have disrespected and hurt God. Maybe we disrespected our parents or a teacher. Maybe we lied to someone. Maybe we refused to go to church or used God's name as a curse word. Yet He still loves us and shows us abundant mercy. Mercy means He did not give us what we deserved. Instead, He took what we deserved upon Himself to save us. That is the love and mercy our mighty God has for us!

Proverbs 8:13–14

¹³ The fear of the LORD is to hate evil;
Pride and arrogance and the evil way
And the perverse mouth I hate.
¹⁴ Counsel is mine, and sound wisdom;
I am understanding, I have strength.

Still another way we are blessed by the fear of God, is that it is like a warning signal to our consciences. Whenever we are tempted to do something wrong or bad, our consciences remind us that we love and fear God. Our consciences help us make right decisions and walk away from negative experiences, experiences that can have lifelong consequences. When we fear the Lord and hate evil, not only are our consciences sensitized, but our hatred

6

for evil is amplified. We simply cannot stand evil things like we did when we walked without God. For example, many believers cannot listen to the same music they listened to before they were saved. This is because the Holy Spirit has sensitized them to what the lyrics say, what they mean, and what they represent. Ungodly and hurtful words, no matter where we hear them or read them, touch our hearts and can lead us astray, but the fear of the Lord helps us turn our eyes and ears away from them.

Proverbs 31:30

30 Charm is deceitful and beauty is passing,
But a woman who fears the LORD, she shall be praised.

A person who fears the Lord stands on the solid rock of trust and faith in Him, and not the shifting sands of the world's promises. This means we do not depend on other people or things—popularity, beauty, money, drugs, alcohol—to give us our joy or peace. Instead, we get those things from our love and fear of God. People will disappoint us, money will disappear, our looks will fade away, but God is never-changing, always present, and is worthy of our praise and obedience. Proverbs 31:30, while it is pictured for us through a woman's beauty, applies to everyone. The promises of the world are all quick to leave us behind, but we will always be praised through our dedication to God.

God's Word in Action

Next Page

Has someone ever encouraged you to lie to your parents, stay out after curfew, or break the law? Did you feel bad about it? God has given us a conscience to help us know right and wrong and help us make good decisions. The next time someone tempts you to do something you shouldn't, consider what God it telling you through your conscience.

Sovereignty

Proverbs 3:5–6

⁵ Trust in the LORD with all your heart,
And lean not on your own understanding;
⁶ In all your ways acknowledge Him,
And He shall direct your paths.

When we say God is sovereign, we mean He has everything under control. It means His plan will work out in the end exactly how He intended it to. Even though we have free will, meaning God has given us the freedom to make our own decisions and choose which path we will walk, the story of creation will end the way He intends it to end. This is one of the great mysteries of God. The Bible tells us to not lean on, or depend on, our own understanding, but to have faith in God and His Word. If we do this, we allow God to surprise us with blessings and miracles.

God, our Father, wants what is best for us, which is to know, love, and serve Him. There is no greater comfort than to allow God to direct our steps. If we aren't careful, we can be enticed away from God by what we see, feel, taste, and hear in this world. God wants us to enjoy all of these things too, but with Him in our hearts.

We can acknowledge God's sovereignty in everything we do, from small things like getting a great parking spot at the grocery store, to big things like making the roster on a school sports team. Thank Him for everything, big and small. We gain unimaginable freedom by putting this level of faith into practice.

Proverbs 16:9

[9] A man's heart plans his way,
But the LORD directs his steps.

Proverbs 20:24

[24] A man's steps are of the LORD;
How then can a man understand his own way?

We can try to direct our own paths and use our free will as a means of independence. The Bible tells us again that God will see His plan come to pass, regardless. He uses our mistakes, fears, doubts, over-eagerness, and hesitations in the same way He uses our courage, discernment, and fear of Him for the advancement of His kingdom. He is sovereign and He is in control, He is perfect and all powerful, and all He desires is your heart! This means He wants a relationship with you. Our God does not love us for what we can give to Him. He loves us because we belong to Him.

Psalm 51:16

[16] For You do not delight in sacrifice, otherwise I would
give it;
You do not take pleasure in burnt offering.

¹⁷ The sacrifices of God are a broken spirit;
A broken and a contrite heart, God, You will not despise.

Even in the Old Testament, before Jesus Christ purchased our salvation on the cross through His sacrifice, the path to God was simple. But the Hebrew people, just as we do today, made salvation complicated. We cannot work to be saved; we can only come to Him with a submissive heart. In God's infinite wisdom and glorious plan to defeat evil once and for all, He paid the price for us through His Son, Jesus Christ. All we have to do is accept this truth in our hearts, which will in turn allow our hearts to be changed, to be turned to Him, by the Holy Spirit.

God's Word in Action

We want to give thanks to God for everything, big and small. What are some things you can thank God for now, that you have not thanked Him for in the past?

Protection

Proverbs 14:26

²⁶ In the fear of the LORD there is strong confidence,
And His children will have a place of refuge.

The Bible tells us that God covers us with His wings (Psalm 91:4), He holds us in His hand (John 10:29), and we are protected under His shadow (Isaiah 49:2). God's Word provides protection in several ways:

- The Word guides, teaches, and directs us
- Spending time in the Bible brings us closer to God
- Knowing the Bible helps us hear the Holy Spirit
- Reading the Bible increases our faith in God

We have no guarantees in this life. No matter how hard we work, how diligent we are, how loyal we are, or how sober-minded we are, in the end it may not all work out the way we want it to. That is the risk we take when we step into this life, full of ambition and hope for the future. But our hope is not in a long life, or comfort, or money, or popularity; it is in God and God alone.

Proverbs 26:17

*¹⁷ He who passes by and meddles in a quarrel not his own
Is like one who takes a dog by the ears.*

The Bible is a guidebook for our lives. The Bible will help us make decisions that will keep us safe and shows us when we are making the correct decisions. God provides a good example for us in Proverbs 26:17. We should not involve ourselves with the arguments of people we don't know, lest we make trouble for ourselves that is not meant to be ours. Often our initial reaction to this situation is to step in and help solve the problem, to mediate. We might want to help, but the Bible tells us otherwise.

Proverbs 14:27

27 The fear of the LORD is a fountain of life,
To turn one away from the snares of death.

God's Word also protects us when we simply spend time reading it. Why? Because we are spending time with God, and we are blessing God with our desire to be with Him. God wants to be with us, and He wants us to seek Him! Spending time with God brings us into a closer relationship with Him, which means we are becoming more intimate with Him. We want to spend time with the people we love, and we want to protect them. God does the same for us because He loves us. Again, remember there are no guarantees, and we accept the will of God no matter the outcome, but God's favor will be upon us. Also, by growing more intimate with God we are connected more intimately with the Holy Spirit. The Holy Spirit communicates with us, and by becoming sensitive to His voice we will be able to discern danger and make better decisions when all the facts are not known.

Psalm 4:8

8 I will both lie down in peace, and sleep:

13

For You alone, O LORD, make me dwell in safety.

As believers in Jesus Christ, it is important that we sit with God every day in prayer and in reading the Bible. Even if we oversleep or have little time, we can honor God by talking to Him and reading a few verses. Developing this habit will bless our spiritual life abundantly and we will carry it into adulthood.

God's Word in Action

Consider Proverbs 26:17 and think of some situations where you would want to stay out of an argument. Then consider where you may need to step into an argument that is not yours? Perhaps if someone your age is arguing with someone much younger?

The Heart of Man

Proverbs 20:6, 9

6 Most men will proclaim each his own goodness,
But who can find a faithful man?
9 Who can say, "I have made my heart clean,
I am pure from my sin"?

Proverbs 27:19

19 As in water face reflects face,
So a man's heart reveals the man.

We tend to think we are much better than we really are. Often, we believe the kindness, generosity, and love in our hearts makes us good people, good enough to get us into heaven. Jesus said in Mark 10:18 that not one of us is good. He said only God alone is good.

This feeling of goodness is one of the reasons some of us find it difficult to come into a relationship with Jesus Christ; we don't think we need Him. The key to growing a strong relationship with Jesus is realizing and confessing that we are sinners. Being a sinner means we think bad thoughts sometimes, misbehave at times, think of our own well-being over the well-being of others, or have desired a possession of another person, to list a few. These are the results of the sinful hearts we are born with.

When Adam and Eve disobeyed God, they decided to do things their own way, instead of having faith in God alone. This got them kicked out of the garden and removed from God's presence. The consequences of Adam's failure have been passed on to every generation after him. This includes us. We have inherited the desire to do things our own way and to be apart from God. This is why each of us, individually, must come to Jesus Christ for redemption.

None of us, not one, can make our hearts clean and pure from sin. It is impossible. Jesus Christ was the only man who could do this because He is God. Think about that, God lived as a man, in the flesh. He experienced what it is like to be tempted in this fallen world. He experienced pain, sorrow, anger, hunger, and thirst. He also experienced friendship, love, fun, family, travel, boating, the countryside, and the city life. He knows us, inside and out, and He is sympathetic to our struggles! We don't have to deny our struggles or hide them. God knows what it is like to live this life, and He wants us to bring our struggles to Him. He can help us, comfort us, and guide us. But coming into this kind of intimacy with God requires that we see the sin we carry in our hearts and come to Jesus for forgiveness and salvation. Jesus cleanses us from sin, removes our guilt, and puts us in right standing with God because He paid the cost of those sins on the cross.

After we are freed from the guilt of sin it is important to remember that every person struggles with the sin nature and that none of us are perfect. Realizing our communal struggle with sin helps us to love more like Jesus and spread the good news of the gospel. When we realize we are as imperfect as everyone else, we can love all people with compassion and understanding, free from judgment. We can love more like Jesus did!

Proverbs 14:12

*12 There is a way that seems right to a man,
But its end is the way of death.*

Proverbs 16:2

*2 All the ways of a man are pure in his own eyes,
But the LORD weighs the spirits.*

Proverbs 16:2 is powerful. So many of us are certain we are doing what is right. We all, believers and nonbelievers, tend to think much too highly of ourselves. But only God knows what is in the heart of any person.

Let that sink in. No matter how well we know a person, or how well others speak of a person, we will never truly know what is in their hearts. We will never know what they are capable of. There are people out there who are not safe to be around. This does not mean we cannot feel safe around certain trusted adults, of course we can, but we must always guard our hearts and our safety. We need to be aware of what is in the hearts of men and women, including our own. This will help us to depend on trusted adults and make better decisions regarding our own actions and safety.

<u>God's Word in Action</u>

The next time you see someone make a mistake or do something selfish, ask yourself if you have the potential to do the same thing.

Chris Long

Protection through God's Word

Pride

Proverbs 16:18

¹⁸ Pride goes before destruction,
And a haughty spirit before a fall.

Pride is a tough topic to deal with because we all feel it, yet the Bible says pride is a sin, period. The sin of pride is when we exalt ourselves, replacing our faith in God with faith in ourselves. In the Bible, pride is almost always connected to haughtiness and arrogance. It suggests lifting ourselves higher than others, bragging about ourselves, and disregarding others in place of self.

Proverbs 21:24

²⁴ A proud and haughty man—"Scoffer" is his name;
He acts with arrogant pride.

Imagine scoring a game-winning goal or playing a difficult piece to perfection at a piano recital. We would feel proud of the accomplishment, right? The pride we feel has two potential sources: either from within ourselves over what we've accomplished, or from God and what He accomplished through the gifts He gave us. When you accomplish something, we can either say, "I did it," or "Isn't God awesome that He gave me this ability and led me to use it for His glory!"

Proverbs 21:24 calls a proud person a scoffer. A scoffer is a person who makes fun of someone or mocks something, which is often something in a religious framework. Now we can see that when we take all the credit for what God has given us, according to Proverbs 21, it is like we are mocking God.

1 Samuel 2:3

[3] "Talk no more so very proudly;
Let no arrogance come from your mouth,
For the LORD is the God of knowledge;
And by Him actions are weighed.

To fight against pride, we must continue to give God the glory for who He has made us to be and for what He has gifted to us. This is a choice we must consciously make. Our parents can say, with honest hearts, they are proud of us. We are their children, and they delight in us the same way God delights in His children (see Psalm 18:19). But parents can't say they are proud of what they have made us into, or proud of the path they have laid out for us, because this is pride that robs God of His glory.

Proverbs 11:2

[2] When pride comes, then comes shame;
But with the humble is wisdom.

The opposite of pride is humility, and we, as believers, strive to be humble. A humble person cannot be haughty or arrogant. Their hearts express love and compassion, which are natural by-products of humility. Humility reminds us that all people—the rich, the homeless, the famous, the convict, and the depressed—come from the same place in the eyes of God, fallen under the curse of sin. No one is better than anyone else, and we all need the saving grace of Jesus Christ. This path of knowing we are not perfect and are not better than any other person, shows us how to love and helps us to love like Jesus loved.

Now we can see why pride brings destruction and shame. Pride focuses on self and takes away the love we have to offer to others. Pride separates us from God and causes us to lose sight of His character and presence, blinding us to our sin and keeping us from repenting to God and seeking Him for our needs, wisdom, peace, and joy.

God's Word in Action

Think about something you have accomplished or are good at that you are proud of. Now consider that God has blessed you with the talent and the opportunity to use it. Practice thanking Him for blessing you with this skill and telling Him you want to honor Him with it.

Greed

Proverbs 11:28

[28] He who trusts in his riches will fall,
But the righteous will flourish like foliage.

The Bible talks about money and the possessions we buy a lot, because God knows money can be a snare for us. It's too easy to depend on it, to put our faith in it, to worship it, and to idolize it. It is easy for us to want all the things it can buy us, like games, toys, bikes, candy, and cool clothes. In reality, having more money doesn't bring peace or security. For many people, having more money leads to spending more money to buy more things. They think these new things will bring them more happiness. This leads to spending more time and money using and maintaining those new things, which leads to a cycle of unhappiness and stress. This cycle has no end when we use our money for the sole purpose of bringing ourselves happiness.

Proverbs 11:24–25

[24] There is one who scatters, yet increases more;
And there is one who withholds more than is right,
But it leads to poverty.
[25] The generous soul will be made rich,
And he who waters will also be watered himself.

Guided by Wisdom

The biblical view of money is the exact opposite of the world's view of money. The world tells us to make as much money as we can, collect as much of it as we can, and buy all the things we want so that we will be secure, happy, and successful. Those are lies. The Bible tells us to have faith in God, that He will provide for us, and to use what He has provided for us to help the poor, broken, and lost. In fact, Proverbs 11:25 says if we do this, we will see an increase and our soul will be made rich. Is it better to have a rich bank account or a rich soul?

In Proverbs 11 God is telling us a spiritual truth: the more we give away, the more we will have. God doesn't promise us earthly riches, wealth, and possessions. Although God may bless us with those things, Proverbs 11 is telling us the more seed we scatter—the more we use our finances, material possessions, and abilities to sow God's Word—then the more we will increase His kingdom. To sacrifice all for God's kingdom is the greatest earthly calling, not to work and stress over money.

Proverbs 23:4–5

4 Do not overwork to be rich;
Because of your own understanding, cease!
5 Will you set your eyes on that which is not?
For riches certainly make themselves wings;
They fly away like an eagle toward heaven.

Proverbs 15:27

²⁷ He who is greedy for gain troubles his own house,
But he who hates bribes will live.

The Bible also warns us against overworking to become rich or trying to become rich quickly. When we overwork to become rich, we lose focus on what is important, like God, family, and service. Of course, we are to be diligent and provide for our basic needs through work, but our focus is not to be on the paycheck only.

God's Word in Action

Look up Proverbs 13:11 and consider how you can have the things you want, like candy or video games, through honest work. Discuss with an adult how earning what you want through honesty can protect your heart from greed.

Jealousy

Proverbs 27:4

4 Wrath is cruel and anger a torrent,
But who is able to stand before jealousy?

Jealousy is a lot like envy, but it involves feelings of inadequacy or threat toward someone else. Jealousy accomplishes nothing because we can't control the person we are jealous of. Fear and jealousy often walk hand-in-hand and may lead to other emotions like anger, withdrawal, depression, violence, or worse.

According to Proverbs 27:4, jealousy can cause more damage than wrath and anger. It is dangerous because it is highly emotional and often irrational. Jealousy causes us to believe things that aren't true, to live in suspicion and distrust, and to want things we may not be able or allowed to have. If we are feeling jealous of the relationship between two other people, or jealous of what someone else has (also called covetousness), then it is important to talk about these feelings with someone we trust, like a parent or teacher. They will be able to advise us on how to process these feelings and how to focus on positive emotions like gratefulness and friendship.

Remember to whom we belong: God. No person, thing, possession, or experience can provide for us the lasting peace and joy that God provides. If we find ourselves in a state of unresolvable jealousy, we may be trying to fill our tank with the wrong fuel. Step back, get into the Word, and tell God what is happening. We should also talk to a trusted adult who can help us through these very sensitive and serious emotions.

We also must be careful if someone else is jealous toward us. This dangerous emotion can cause people to do illogical or even cruel things. Look at the proverb again. Wrath and anger can cause some serious outcomes, but jealousy has the most potential for danger and destruction. This is alarming and God is giving us a strong warning about this emotion.

<u>God's Word in Action</u>

Start keeping a journal to record your relationship with God, your successes and struggles in life, and your feelings. Write how God and your relationship with Him influences your interactions, feelings, and responses.

Anger

Proverbs 14:29

[29] He who is slow to wrath has great understanding,
But he who is impulsive exalts folly.

Anger is poison to a person's soul. Its root is found in bitterness and unforgiveness. As Proverbs 14:29 says, one can be slow to wrath. This is not only a choice, but it is also a response to discipline. Sometimes we are able to see anger coming and choose not to let it take hold of us and control the situation. But those moments are rare. Anger can flare up quickly—in an instant—before we are able to think the situation through properly. It can cause you to lose control. The emotion of anger, when turned inward, can cause us to withdraw or harm ourselves. When turned outward anger can turn into vandalism, violence, or lashing out with hurtful words. These responses can be done with forethought or impulsively, either way, we must be able to control anger.

To become a young man or a young woman who is "slow to wrath," we must intentionally practice that discipline. Often, when we are wronged by a bully, hurt by a friend or a stranger, the best way to deal with anger is to choose not to react until we have taken some time to think about what just happened. This allows us to cool down and often we will realize the situation is not as serious as we first thought. It also allows us to think about how we will respond to the wrong committed against us. It gives us time to bring the problem before God in prayer and to discuss it with a parent or a friend. Then we can respond under control, with God and good counsel to support us.

It is also important to forgive those who have wronged us. This can be a process, and at times can require strong spiritual discipline and dependence on God's grace to allow us to truly forgive someone who has done harm to us. The key to learning forgiveness is to continue to seek God through His Word, the Bible, and to talk to trusted adults about our faith.

Proverbs 16:32

[32] He who is slow to anger is better than the mighty,
And he who rules his spirit than he who takes a city.

This is important. One who is slow to anger is mightier, meaning more capable and successful, than the mightiest of men in strength and skill. The ability to control anger has a direct link to success as a young adult. Developing a temperament that is slow to anger is part of our pursuit for wisdom. Being slow to anger allows us to make clearer decisions, earn the favor of our peers and superiors, and maintain important relationships.

Finally, remember anger itself is not a sin. Anger is a valid human emotion. If we see injustice, we are to be angered by it. When God's name is misused, then we are to be angered by it. Anger becomes sin when we react to it with violence or hateful words rather than in love and patience. Sometimes aggressive action will be required, like when Jesus flipped the tables and drove out the vendors in the temple courts with a homemade whip! This story is hard for us to understand, but it validates for us that when we see injustice, or a wrong committed toward God, we must be willing to act.

<u>God's Word in Action</u>

Think of the last time you became angry and acted on it. Replay that scene in your mind and show yourself how you could have reacted differently to avoid the anger you expressed.

Debt

Proverbs 22:7

[7] The rich rules over the poor,
And the borrower is servant to the lender.

A debt is something owed to someone else and is commonly associated with money and financial loans. We can also be in debt to someone by word or deed, by making promises or being expected to return a favor, but in this chapter we are talking about owing money. Besides, if we are living as true Christians, we will never feel that someone owes us anything because we did them a favor. With the help of the Holy Spirit, we serve others through the love in our hearts and not for personal gain. Likewise, when someone helps us out of their own free will, while we may want to do something nice for them to show our appreciation, we shouldn't feel indebted to them. We know in our hearts that if an opportunity arises to serve them in the future, we will do it. We find this biblical teaching in Philippians 2, verse 3.

> [3] *Let nothing be done through selfish ambition or conceit, but in lowliness of mind let each esteem others better than himself.*

There is a claim in the business world that "smart," or "good" debt exists. This means a person can earn more money with proper debt management, as opposed to earning less money

31

if the debt, or loan, was not taken on in the first place. For example, a trash hauling business that used a two-door passenger car to haul the trash would be very inefficient, not to mention unhygienic. The business would probably buy a truck to haul the trash as soon as possible. Then they could haul more trash per trip to the landfill and save time and money. The common practice today is to take out a loan to purchase this truck, then to repay the loan as the truck earned more profits. This is what is meant by "smart" or "good" debt. Likewise, it is the cultural norm today for most people to take out a loan, or a mortgage, to buy their first home (most people carry this debt for the rest of their lives). These are considered justifiable things to do by both Christian and secular financial advisers, because they increase, or at least, maintain wealth.

There is nothing inherently good about debt and the word of God says what it says on the subject: that debt is bad. Period. The Bible likens debt to slavery, where the borrower is enslaved to the lender. This is because when we are in debt to someone, we have voluntarily given them power over us. This power may not be revealed in a coercive manner, where the lender is able to manipulate us, but it will always exist beneath the surface as long as the debt exists. We will always owe that person or institution something to the point where they may take back our belongings if we fail to make the payments.

To buy a truck or house without taking on debt requires sacrifice, patience, and wisdom. It will require the wisdom to think ahead and save money up front. Then we need patience, because it will take time to save a large sum of money. Finally, sacrifices will have to be made. It is hard to save money for a future investment if we cannot let go of some luxuries, like a few trips to the movie theater, or eating in restaurants, or in biblical times, going without olive oil for a while.

This society tries to trick us into thinking debt is normal, but it is not; it is literally bondage. In our society credit card debt is responsible for the destruction of lives and entire families. The added stress of having possessions we can't pay for doesn't come close to justifying the value of that item we own on credit. Never, ever, go into debt with credit cards. Never go into debt to buy big items like furniture, electronics, motorcycles, boats, and cars. When we do this we will realize we have no financial peace until the debt is paid off.

The only debt that is worth taking on is for what was mentioned before: to finance a business or to buy a family a home. But remember, when we do that, our focus must be to pay these loans off before we even think about dream vacations or buying luxury items we don't need.

We must also guard our assets from wasteful depletion. Many people spend hundreds of dollars per month without even realizing it because they have too many monthly subscriptions to streaming, gaming, and shopping services.

God's Word in Action

Next Page

Pretend you could buy a new bike for $10 to replace the bike you already have, but $10 was all the money you had. If you bought the new bike you would have to spend $1 per week to put air in the tires and water in your water bottle. Your old bike does not have this expense. How would buying this new bike affect you in the future?

Fools

Proverbs 25:19

[19] Confidence in an unfaithful man in time of trouble
Is like a bad tooth and a foot out of joint.

Proverbs 14:15

[15] The simple believes every word,
But the prudent considers well his steps.

Calling someone a fool is very strong and offensive, and we should not use the word loosely. Foolish people do exist and, given the abundance of proverbs that educate us about fools, it is clearly a topic worth discussing without sugarcoating it. First, based on the proverbs selected for this chapter, what is a fool? Fools are unfaithful, meaning they can't be trusted. They are simple and they tend to believe anything they are told, in other words, they don't think things through. They are not humble and are likely double-minded. They make jokes about and make fun of things they don't understand, and they never learn or change their behavior. Finally, they are wicked, meaning they have rejected God and His wisdom.

Second, how do we not act foolishly? Being a fool is not a question of intelligence. The issues of foolishness are thinking, being responsible, and making good decisions. A person who acts foolishly tends to act impulsively and selfishly. They only think as far ahead as the next sentence they are about to speak. Often, having fun is more important than being responsible and safe. Also, people who act foolishly tend not to consider the advice given to them by friends and family members. They simply do what they want to do. Most of the time it is beneficial to at least consider the advice we are given, even if we choose not to follow it. This is part of thinking through challenges and problems in life.

Proverbs 9:7–9

[7] "He who corrects a scoffer gets shame for himself,
And he who rebukes a wicked man only harms himself.
[8] Do not correct a scoffer, lest he hate you;
Rebuke a wise man, and he will love you.
[9] Give instruction to a wise man, and he will be still wiser;
Teach a just man, and he will increase in learning.

As Proverbs 9:9 tells us, we want to be wise. A wise person will consider what he or she hears or reads and will think about it. A wise person will seek advice from others and will listen to the advice that is given to them. A wise person is always learning and trying to do things better. Finally, a wise person seeks the wisdom and the will of God by spending time with Him in His Word and in prayer.

<u>God's Word in Action</u>

Think of a time when someone you trusted gave you advice and you did not even consider it, only to realize the advice given would have been very helpful to you had you have taken it. Remember, it is almost always good to think through the advice you are given, even if you choose not to follow the advice.

Alcohol

Proverbs 20:1

[1] Wine is a mocker,
Strong drink is a brawler,
And whoever is led astray by it is not wise.

Alcohol has been in use for thousands of years. It was consumed in biblical times and is written about in the Bible. Jesus's first public miracle was when He turned water into wine for a wedding (John 2:7–10), and it was recommended for use as a medicine for the stomach and as an anti-stressor (1 Timothy 5:23 and Psalm 104:14–15). Alcohol can also create negative and shameful situations with catastrophic consequences because it impairs our judgment, causes us to lose control, and can allow other people to take advantage of us. Because alcohol is shown to have some benefits while also being dangerous, people are divided on how to approach the topic of alcohol.

In our chapter verse, God is telling us that alcohol leads us astray. That means it distracts us from what is important, like loving others and doing what is good. It can cause us to lose sight of God's will for our lives. The Bible tells us the person who is led astray by alcohol is not wise. This means that using alcohol is a foolish thing to do.

Proverbs 31:4–5

⁴ It is not for kings, O Lemuel,
It is not for kings to drink wine,
Nor for princes intoxicating drink;
⁵ Lest they drink and forget the law,
And pervert the justice of all the afflicted.

In Proverbs 31 God is warning our leaders not to drink alcohol. We can see the potential results are significant. We can forget God's law when we drink and make poor decisions that can harm others.

Proverbs 21:17

¹⁷ He who loves pleasure will be a poor man;
He who loves wine and oil will not be rich.

Let's not be naïve about alcohol. It is a drug that changes the way we feel and think when we use it. It can cause serious problems and it robs us of our possessions. Using alcohol can rob us of our time and money through drunkenness, accidents, and arrests. It may cause violence and destroy relationships. It encourages poor decision making, and it desensitizes us while we are under its influence. Some people become addicted to it and can't stop drinking it, even after it has destroyed their lives.

<u>God's Word in Action</u>

Make a plan you can use if you find yourself in a situation where you are being pressured to use alcohol. Be prepared to say no and stand under the pressure, and know beforehand who you can call to come pick you up.

Corruption

Proverbs 4:14–17

[14] Do not enter the path of the wicked,
And do not walk in the way of evil.
[15] Avoid it, do not travel on it;
Turn away from it and pass on.
[16] For they do not sleep unless they have done evil;
And their sleep is away unless they make someone fall.
[17] For they eat the bread of wickedness,
And drink the wine of violence.

An incorrupt heart does not exist. We are all born with sin and into a sinful world that encourages us to walk in the ways of sin and evil. Even if we don't actively participate in cruelty or crime, we all possess the desire to serve 'self' first and foremost, and that is sin.

But thank God for His wisdom and perfection, because in all this confusion, temptation, and turmoil, He has given us a beautiful gift—the gift of choice. In Proverbs 4:14–15, God is telling us to choose our path and to choose it wisely. We also learn in verses 16–17 a lot about the evil heart and the person who embraces that wicked calling. The Lord tells us they eat and drink wickedness and violence, which means they live and breathe it, they are totally overcome by it, and they are unable to make their

41

way in this world apart from it. The absence of evil deeds in their daily routine causes them to lose sleep!

Proverbs 1:10

[10] My son, if sinners entice you,
Do not consent.

Those who pursue an evil path want company. They want to bring people with them, into the pits of hell, if they even believe in such a place. Their ways of sin can be tempting; they boast about how much fun they have and they brag on themselves. We all are tempted. It is the natural inclination of our hearts to exalt self. But again, we have a choice. If an evil person entices us, we do not have to consent! Enticement, or temptation, is not the sin. The sin is when we consent to, agree with, and participate in evil activities.

God will show us the path we have chosen is the better way, but we have to have faith in Him. We have to have faith that it is better to serve Him than it is to serve the world.

Proverbs 23:17

[17] Do not let your heart envy sinners,
But be zealous for the fear of the LORD all the day.

We must guard our hearts against envying a person who has comfort, success, and pleasure through and in sin. Our reward is not in this world, it waits for us in heaven. If we trust in God, He will not fail us. We will experience a full and happy life in the service of God. All the money in the world cannot compare to the reward of Heaven. God is the one who provides our needs and fulfills our lives, not worldly rewards.

God's Word in Action

Look up and meditate on Proverbs 25:5 and 10:9. Ask yourself, "How can I recognize a person whose intent is evil or selfish?"

Safety

Proverbs 22:3

³ A prudent man foresees evil and hides himself,
But the simple pass on and are punished.

Beware of those who tell us not to worry about our own well-being. Some people claim that taking proper precautions against harm or evil is a sign of a lack of true faith. They will cite Bible verses that clearly speak those words, like Matthew 6, which tells us not to worry about what we will eat tomorrow, or where we will find shelter, for God will provide, and He will. Jesus is not telling us to not work or plan ahead. If you read the whole chapter, you will see He is telling us not to worry. Psalm 91, the psalm of protection, is also cited as a claim to not protect ourselves. It says God will protect us in the midst of war, from disease, from plagues, from wild animals, and from tripping over a stone. We should have no doubt God will do that for His children if it is His will. What we must remember is that we are to read and consider the entire Bible to fully understand what each passage is telling us. We must know the Word of God, and to do that we must read it every day, then we can determine the best course of action in any given situation.

Proverbs 22:3 tells us that the responsible person sees evil coming and gets out of the way, and that it is foolish to walk aimlessly through life without any awareness of our surroundings.

44

In fact, this proverb is repeated twice in the book, word for word! The second appearance is in Proverbs 27:12.

Our God is a God of action. Besides telling us to protect ourselves, this proverb is also telling us to be proactive and not to simply sit idle and allow God to take care of everything. It tells us we are responsible for the actions we choose to take or choose not to take.

Psalm 119:105

[105] Thy word is a lamp unto my feet, and a light unto my path.

If we go into the forest at night, would we take a flashlight? It would be wise to do so and would increase our safety on the rugged and unfamiliar trail. God's Word, when we know it, does the same for us in life, and we can live our lives by it. We become like one walking around in the dark with a flashlight. When we spend time alone reading the Bible every day, even if we only have a few minutes, it becomes our flashlight in life.

God's Word in Action

Plan ways to keep yourself safe when you go to school or to the park. Maybe it is going with a friend or letting your parents know where you are at all times.

Chris Long

Growing Character through God's Word

Humility

Proverbs 22:1, 4

¹ A good name is to be chosen rather than great riches,
Loving favor rather than silver and gold.

⁴ By humility and the fear of the LORD
Are riches and honor and life.

Being humble means we place others above ourselves. This is an act of love, and it follows God's law when He tells us to love our neighbors as ourselves and to consider others before ourselves (Matthew 22:39 and Philippians 2:3). In respect to God, humility gives us a sense of our own unworthiness. In fearful respect we see God as perfect and all powerful. He is self-created and is our Creator and Redeemer. In all His power God loves us very much. He desires us to be humble in His presence and to be humble within His creation. When we show humility, we are honoring God.

Plus, according to our chapter verse, Proverbs 22, the benefits of humility are to be desired. In humility we earn a good name, which is better than silver and gold. When we are humble in the sight of God we find riches, honor, and life. Isn't God wonderful, in that the traits He desires for us often have the potential for great earthly reward? This is what the Bible gives us, everything we need to live a holy and righteous life, which is a life of reward. Not necessarily in money, relationships, or relaxation, but freedom from anxiety, anger, depression, pride, and fear of death.

Proverbs 29:23

23 A man's pride will bring him low,
But the humble in spirit will retain honor.

Proverbs 18:12

12 Before destruction the heart of a man is haughty,
And before honor is humility.

These verses show us that humility offers us honor, while pride leads to destruction. It is interesting when we look back in history and study the rise and fall of great nations, like the fall of ancient Rome in 476 AD, or of large corporations, like the collapse of Enron in 2001, we easily see the warning flags of moral decay, selfishness, and greed. Often, when people are building and creating new visions like businesses or nations, the focus is on the good it will produce, like protection or better jobs. But, like Proverbs 18:12 says, when the nation or company fails, a loss of humility, or a loss of the vision of the greater good, can be seen.

Proverbs 25:6–7

6 Do not exalt yourself in the presence of the king,
And do not stand in the place of the great;
7 For it is better that he say to you, "Come up here,"
Than that you should be put lower in the presence of the

prince,
Whom your eyes have seen.

Humility frees us from the struggle of trying to be someone of importance in the eyes of men. It gives a heart to honor God instead. When we try to please other people to create our value we are taking that honor away from God. It is the humble spirit, submitted to God, that will raise us up in honor with our fellow man, not a proud one.

Finally, it is important to mention that humility is not something we fake or seek out only when personal gain is likely. Being a humble person is genuine and is a condition of our hearts. To maintain a humble character, we must look to God and continually give Him the glory.

God's Word in Action

Read the description of God's throne room in Revelation 4. Is this a vision that causes you to respond with humility?

Generosity

Proverbs 14:31

³¹ He who oppresses the poor reproaches his Maker,
But he who honors Him has mercy on the needy.

G od desires us to help and care for the poor among us. We are
to use what God has blessed us with to bless others. In
Matthew 25:40 Jesus said, "Assuredly, I say to you, inasmuch as
you did it to one of the least of these My brethren, you did it to
Me." Jesus said what Proverbs 14:31 says: when we help people
in need, we are serving Him directly! The opposite is also true:
when we wrong or hurt another person, we are hurting God
directly.

Proverbs 21:13

*¹³ Whoever shuts his ears to the cry of the poor
Will also cry himself and not be heard.*

Proverbs 22:9

*⁹ He who has a generous eye will be blessed,
For he gives of his bread to the poor.*

Proverbs 29:7

7 The righteous considers the cause of the poor,
But the wicked does not understand such knowledge.

God speaks about the poor and His heart for them often in His Word. He knows we live in a fallen world, and because Jesus lived with us on the earth, we know God is sensitive to the troubles we experience. He knows some will have opportunities that others will not. He knows some of us will make bad decisions, and others will have bad things happen to them that are out of their control. It is God's desire that we love one another, and this is what that love looks like: caring for others in need and giving from what we have.

God tells us if we ignore or misuse the poor and broken, then He will ignore us, and poverty awaits us. The word poverty here doesn't necessarily speak in monetary terms, but certainly in spiritual terms. When we turn a blind eye to those in need our conscience suffers, our hearts are hardened, and we become more self-focused. All of these can damage our relationship with God.

There are many ways we can give back to the poor in our communities, even if we don't have money to offer. We can volunteer at a food pantry or a homeless shelter. Or we can organize a fundraiser and give the money raised to a charity. God has made us to be creative people. This frees us to work beyond what is in our piggy banks.

God's Word in Action

As already mentioned, there are many ways we can show generosity without requiring money. Make a list of ways you can be generous to those in need with the talents, skills, and ideas God has given to you.

Self-Control

Proverbs 19:11

¹¹ The discretion of a man makes him slow to anger,
And his glory is to overlook a transgression.

Every action we take, whether out of anger, haste, or contentment, has one thing in common—we chose to take that action. *Discretion* is the ability to respond without causing offense or revealing private information. It also means we are aware that the actions we take will likely influence the direction in which a given situation progresses. Proverbs 19:11 is about making choices that deny our selfish desires. These are the hardest choices to make correctly because everything inside us is telling us to take revenge, to show how angry we are, or to at least make sure the other person knows they messed up. Even when anger is not involved, often we are tempted to demonstrate how smart and awesome we are, again, at the risk of causing offense through our pride.

When we exercise self-control, we choose not to act on our anger and frustration, even if our rights were violated by someone else. Exhibiting self-control allows us to own the situation and stay in control of our emotions. A peacemaker (Matthew 5:9) is someone who is able to lead others to a place of reconciliation and peace. It's impossible to always avoid conflict, embarrassment, or aggravation, but we do not have to let them control us.

Whenever we are in a situation that is threatening to spin out of control, we should look to God for help. A quick prayer, saying simply, "God help me find the best way to navigate this problem," helps us draw on the power of God and His Holy Spirit. God will help us control our emotions when we look to Him. He will bring to remembrance past situations to help us navigate the current situation. He also gives us new ideas and fresh guidance, to help us maintain our self-control.

If possible, sometimes the best way to maintain self-control is to momentarily step away from the situation. This allows us more time to pray, to think the situation through, and to gain control of our emotions.

Proverbs 25:28

[28] *Whoever has no rule over his own spirit*
Is like a city broken down, without walls.

A person without self-control is vulnerable. A lack of self-control makes us prone to making mistakes and opens the door for us to hurt people unnecessarily and sometimes irreparably. If we notice we are losing our self-control, then it is important to step back and regain it. Stop the conversation, leave the room, go outside; whatever it takes to find a moment to regain that control.

The art of self-control is a life skill God can use. It is a skill we can meditate on, practice, and improve.

God's Word in Action

One of the best ways to exhibit self-control is to simply not speak. Can you recall a situation when you "spoke your mind," and in doing so caused anger or offense to take root in another person. Consider how if you had remained quiet until you were able to think of a positive and constructive response, how differently the situation would have turned out.

Sympathy

Proverbs 27:7

[7] A satisfied soul loathes the honeycomb,
But to a hungry soul every bitter thing is sweet.

Always remember we are not to judge the actions, or inactions, of another, because we do not know what is happening in their hearts. We don't know what they have experienced in their lives or what has conditioned them to behave in ways we do not understand. The human mind is extremely complex, and this complexity can cause confusion, can lead to manipulation, and can result in poor decision making.

It is hard for us to see people in bad situations, like homelessness or abusive relationships. It is even more difficult if we believe they are not willing to do anything to change their bad situation. God is explaining this to us in Proverbs 27:7. In the first part of the verse He tells us when we are well off and taken care of, when all our needs are met, we can start to dislike luxuries. We can actually tire of eating too much honey!

But look at the second part of the verse; "…to a hungry soul every bitter thing is sweet." This person's soul is so hungry to have his or her needs met, that they find fulfillment of their needs in negative, unhealthy, or otherwise horrible situations. What is bitter to us might appear fulfilling to a poor soul who has not been loved or appreciated the way we have been. Therefore, when we see someone who is in a bad relationship and they do nothing to get out of it, or someone who is addicted to drugs or alcohol, we are not to judge. Never judge another for their faults. Rather be sympathetic! We must find sympathy inside of us for those who are hurting, even if we don't immediately feel it in our hearts. God will give us hearts of sympathy for the hurting, the addicted, the poor, and the lost, if we ask Him. There are many people in the world who are desperately trying to scrape little bits of joy out of negativity and pain. What they need is a sympathetic and listening ear, not another judge telling them what they should do now or what they shouldn't have done in the past.

Empathy is even stronger and more powerful than sympathy. Sympathy represents feelings of sadness, pity, and compassion for someone. To be empathetic means we can put ourselves into the position of another who is hurting or in pain. Empathy means we *share* in the other person's pain, which creates a deeper bond of love between the two and will open the flood gates for the Holy Spirit to work through us in that person's life.

This is how Jesus loved us. All of us are imperfect and not one of us deserves the honor of standing before the throne of God (Romans 3:23). If we can see our own imperfections and realize Jesus loves us despite of our selfishness and sinful tendencies, then we can learn to love like Jesus did, without judging and with empathy. Pride will tell us we are better than an addict, or a homeless person, or an atheist, but that is not so. We are not better than anyone in the eyes of God, for He loves us all the same and desires that all of us can come into His glory through His Son, Jesus.

1 Timothy 2:3–4

[3] For this is good and acceptable in the sight of God our Savior, [4] who desires all men to be saved and to come to the knowledge of the truth.

God's Word in Action

Reach out and do something genuinely kind for someone who is in need, maybe a classmate. Do it without the expectations of getting something in return. It can be as simple as a smile and a hello in the hallway.

Courage

Proverbs 24:10

[10] If you faint in the day of adversity,
Your strength is small.

Courage is not a feeling. Courage is how we act regardless of how we are feeling. We all experience fear. It's part of life. Overcoming fear and being courageous is what we must pursue. When we put our faith in God, we can overcome fear and not be controlled by it. This frees us to develop traits that honor God, like courage, humility, and love.

When all we want to do is run away, there is one thing we must do first: ask God for help. We are never alone, even when we stand alone. King David, in Ziklag before he became king (see 1 Samuel 30), had everything stolen from him. His own people wanted to kill him because of it, but the first thing he did was ask God for strength. He didn't muster up the courage he needed to act, he didn't make plans, he didn't try to appease his people, he went to God. He went to battle on the spiritual level before he went into physical battle.

Learn how to fight.

Not with our fists. Hopefully there won't be much need for that in our lives. We must learn how to fight to attain the goals we've set for ourselves. When we are working toward a goal and everything seems to be against us, *don't give up!* If we make it a habit to fight for our dreams and goals, our courage and strength will increase, little by little, through practice. When that day of adversity arrives we won't faint because we have learned courage. We did not let quitting become a habit in our lives. When we set high goals and fight to reach them, we become strong because of it.

Courage is not the opposite of humility. Rather, these two wonderful traits complement and strengthen each other. We can be courageous when we are terrified, we can ask God for strength, we can act on what we know is right, and we can thank God for the outcome. A courageous and humble warrior will move mountains for God's kingdom. We can show love and compassion for those who are hurting, spot injustice in disguise, and practice courage in action, regardless of the personal consequence.

God's Word in Action

Think about the last time you were too afraid to act. In retrospect, what should you have done? What will it take to act with courage the next time?

Honesty

Proverbs 28:13

¹³ He who covers his sins will not prosper,
But whoever confesses and forsakes them will have mercy.

Sometimes being honest is hard. It is the nature of the selfish heart to cover up our mistakes and crimes. We have all told lies to avoid trouble or shame or kept quiet when we should have confessed to something.

Proverbs 28:21

²¹ To show partiality is not good,
Because for a piece of bread a man will transgress.

We all make mistakes—every one of us. Imperfection is a universal trait. That is why we need a savior, because evil and sin cannot stand in the presence of God. Jesus took the penalty of our sin, and in doing so, He made it possible for us to stand before God. God will forgive our sins because Jesus paid for them. Our tendency to be dishonest is one of the more obvious ways we all sin and fall short of perfection. It is easy to do and it is often effective. Proverbs 28:21 tells us being dishonest is so easy that we'll do it for a piece of bread.

Proverbs 19:5

[5] A false witness will not go unpunished,
And he who speaks lies will not escape.

Dishonesty is a sin, and there are consequences, even if we happen to not get caught. For one, it bothers our consciences. When we lie and have deceived someone, we feel bad about it. We know we have done wrong and while we may have avoided trouble for ourselves, we likely passed that trouble on to someone else who didn't deserve it. That is selfish. God hears every lie, and lying will not go unpunished. We don't always get caught, but we will always be punished because our consciences won't let us off free and clear. There is always a spiritual consequence to sin.

We will face temptations to be dishonest all our lives. Sometimes it won't seem to matter if the truth is known or not. In fact, it may appear to be beneficial to everyone if the truth is hidden away forever. But we live in a dishonest world and adding more dishonesty to it makes our world a darker place. When we live with the Spirit of God in our hearts, then our hearts will desire to do the right thing, even when it is the hard thing. By focusing on the word of God we become sensitive to even the smallest sins, which are often simple little lies. A half-truth is a whole lie.

God's Word in Action

Think of a recent occurrence when you were dishonest, maybe you told a lie to your parents. Repent to God and ask His forgiveness. If possible, do the same with your parents.

Peace

Proverbs 17:14

¹⁴ The beginning of strife is like releasing water;
Therefore stop contention before a quarrel starts.

Paul said, "If it is possible, as much as depends on you, live peaceably with all men" (Romans 12:18). Arguments erupt all the time because we are all looking out for our self-interests. Sometimes we can avoid petty arguments and quarrels. Other times we choose to overlook offenses and walk away.

When we argue and fight, we say things that we would not say otherwise. Anger causes us to lose control. We become angry when our personal interests are threatened. Like water released from behind a dam, words flow, and the argument escalates into a potentially damaging situation. Anger and self-interest destroy peace and cause division.

Jesus prayed to His Father that we would be united and not divided, in John 17.

²⁰ "I do not pray for these alone, but also for those who will believe in Me through their word; ²¹ that they all may be one, as You, Father, are in Me, and I in You; that they also may be one in Us that the world may believe that You sent Me."

God helps us further by adding this verse in James 1:

[19] So then, my beloved brethren, let every man be swift to hear, slow to speak, slow to wrath;

We can see that it is God's will for us to be united as brothers and sisters in Christ and to live in peace with one another. God gives us the tools to do that, many of which are found in this book. They are love, humility, forgiveness, and verses like James 1:19.

Proverbs 20:3

[3] It is honorable for a man to stop striving,
Since any fool can start a quarrel.

Sometimes we won't be able to avoid an argument. It is honorable to search for common ground and a peaceful solution.

The types of arguments we want to participate in are called debates. Quarrels emerge from anger and conflict. Debates take place with the understanding that the parties involved have a different point of view on a subject. The opposing sides are aware that each will have time to present their argument. It is controlled and respectful. Each side is listened to.

When all is said and done and the debating is over, we must remember our peace is found in God alone. On those grounds we can be humble and peaceful with our friends and neighbors.

<u>God's Word in Action</u>

How can we learn to debate an issue with our friends and acquaintances, instead of simply quarreling?

Faithfulness

Proverbs 3:21–24

21 My son, let them not depart from your eyes—
Keep sound wisdom and discretion;
22 So they will be life to your soul
And grace to your neck.
23 Then you will walk safely in your way,
And your foot will not stumble.
24 When you lie down, you will not be afraid;
Yes, you will lie down and your sleep will be sweet.

So many of us grow up and rush into the open arms of the world, eager to experience its sights, tastes, smells, and touches. It is a natural response to young adulthood, the call to adventure and the taste of freedom. God wants us to have the best of what His creation has to offer. He is God and He is Creator, and everything is His. Everything He made is good.

Proverbs 14:14

14 The backslider in heart will be filled with his own ways,
But a good man will be satisfied from above.

Why, when young people leave their homes and take their place in the world, do they so often choose to leave God behind?

Guided by Wisdom

Why are they so quick to believe that carrying God's Word in their hearts will limit the enjoyment of His creation?

This is a lie of the devil, to lead us to believe that enjoyment is not meant for God's children. God's Spirit in our hearts makes everything good available to us.

We can enjoy the foods that are set before us, the arts that are presented to us, and God's people of all ethnicities, beliefs, and backgrounds. We, as believers, are a light in this world, and as Matthew 5:14–16 tells us, our light is not to be hidden. It is to shine forth for all to see. To be a light that allows all those we meet to be able to see through the darkness that has blinded them. This is our calling, and it is as simple as keeping the word of God written on our hearts, bound around our necks, and never forsaken.

Of course, there is a limit to that. If something is being done in the name of evil, darkness, or of the demonic, then we refuse to partake. This refusal is done as a sign that we are children of God, and we love and respect Him and His name. It is not because we fear we may lose our salvation, but simply because we are called to stand apart.

Enjoy the beauty of God and all His creation. He will guide us and protect us, warning us by the Spirit when something isn't right about a situation. In those cases, watch your back, put up your guard, and be ready to respond or run away if something isn't right. In all cases we are guided by the Holy Spirit.

Proverbs 28:9

[9] One who turns away his ear from hearing the law,
Even his prayer is an abomination.

The Bible urges us to stand firm in our faith because God knows we are facing evil in this life. This evil comes in the form of temptation, doubt, and lies. There will be times, even seasons, when we don't feel strong in our faith, but keep up the good fight and don't let go of what you've been given. Refuse to give up this precious gift, our faith. Keep it. Keep the faith!

Proverbs 3:3–4

[3] Let not mercy and truth forsake you;
Bind them around your neck,
Write them on the tablet of your heart,
[4] And so find favor and high esteem
In the sight of God and man.

God's Word in Action

Read 1 Corinthians 10:18–33. Consider what Paul is saying about the freedom of those who are believers in Jesus Christ. In your journal, list some activities you feel are not right for a follower of Jesus to partake in and discuss it with a parent or another trusted adult.

Love

Proverbs 25:21–22

²¹ If your enemy is hungry, give him bread to eat;
And if he is thirsty, give him water to drink;
²² For so you will heap coals of fire on his head,
And the Lord will reward you.

God has called us to love everyone, even those we don't like. If we help our enemies when they are in need then He will reward us and cause frustration to them in the process. Our prayer is that this frustration will lead them to consider God in their lives through our love and kindness.

Who are our enemies? They can look quite different depending on what lifestyle we live, where we live, and what is happening socially around us at the time. If we are in a gang our enemies might pretend to be "family" while trying to force us to do something illegal. If we play on a sports team, then our "enemies" will be our competitors. When we are active and outspoken followers of Christ, our enemies may seek to damage our character and reputation.

But we are called to love all these people. Why? Our sin has created an opposition in us toward God (see Romans 8:7), meaning we have been His enemies, but God has always loved us (see 1 John 4:19). Therefore, we are to love our enemies the same way He loves us. When Jesus was tortured, ridiculed, and executed, He confirmed His love for the people who had done those things to Him by asking God to forgive them (see Luke 23:34). Those people include you and me, because even though we were not present at Jesus's crucifixion, we have the same selfish and sinful tendencies they had.

God desires for us to have the same heart of love and forgiveness for our enemies that Jesus has. Jesus tells us plainly, "love your enemies and pray for those who persecute you, that you may be children of your Father in heaven. He causes his sun to rise on the evil and the good, and sends rain on the righteous and the unrighteous" (Matthew 5:44–45 NIV). He doesn't say what we'd prefer Him to say, which is to just let them be and not bother them, but to *love* them.

Proverbs 24:17–18

17 Do not rejoice when your enemy falls,
And do not let your heart be glad when he stumbles;
18 Lest the LORD see it, and it displease Him,
And He turn away His wrath from him.

When we are happy with our enemy's failure, we are in the wrong because we are indulging in pride and arrogance. We are also expressing joy over someone else's pain and disappointment. God may even reverse our enemies' fortunes, which suggests a fall may now be coming our way if we rejoice in another's failure.

God's Word in Action

Do you have friends that attend a competing school? If not, ask yourself why? What are some ways you can reach out and show a loving interest in them?

Chris Long

God's Word in Everyday Life

Evangelism

Proverbs 24:11–12

¹¹ Deliver those who are drawn toward death,
And hold back those stumbling to the slaughter.
¹² If you say, "Surely we did not know this,"
Does not He who weighs the hearts consider it?
He who keeps your soul, does He not know it?
And will He not render to each man according to his deeds?

Proverbs 24:11 describes those who do not know God and who are walking into an eternity in hell. As believers their destinies should frighten us, and their current state of unbelief should break our hearts. Jesus lifts our earthly burdens and replaces them with love, joy, and peace. His greatest gift is salvation, and he gives us wisdom to understand what that means. We must be courageous and find ways to tell others about Him.

We cannot use ignorance as an excuse because God knows our hearts. He knows what we know, what we feel, and why we do what we do. We can lie and deceive ourselves, but we can't deceive God.

When we decide to tell others about Jesus, we don't have to stand in church and give a sermon, or walk up to strangers on the street and confidently proclaim His name, or be a full-time missionary. Some of us may be good at those things, and some of us may be terrified by them. We all have been blessed with different gifts, which means we will each have our own way to tell someone else about Jesus. Here are some ways you can be a good witness to Christ and open doors to conversations with people about Him.

- Volunteer at a food pantry, soup kitchen, or homeless shelter

- Use creative talents to express God's love and glory through painting, poetry, or music

- People will see that we don't lie, drink, or swear and ask us why, tell them

- When you meet someone and you sense sadness or pain in their life, ask them questions and listen

- No matter what job you find to do, do it well, as if Jesus is looking over your shoulder

Regardless of what we do or the talent we are blessed with, we can use them to serve our Creator and shine His light. The more we practice, the more our comfort zone grows. Taking the first step to talk to someone about Jesus is the hardest. But like every other skill, it gets easier with practice.

God's Word in Action

Read Jesus' Great Commission in Matthew 28, verses 19 and 20. He tells us to tell the nations about Him. How many nations are represented in your classroom or school?

Power of Words

Proverbs 15:4

⁴ A wholesome tongue is a tree of life,
But perverseness in it breaks the spirit.

The words we say have power. When we speak positive words, we are building up ourselves and the person receiving those words. Likewise, when we speak negative words, we crush our own spirit and the spirit of the listener. Have you ever heard a person yell at someone unjustly or belittle them with their words, and even though you weren't involved you felt your heart break? This is the truth of Proverbs 15:4 moving inside you.

Jesus said, "But those things which proceed out of the mouth come from the heart, and they defile a man" (Matthew 15:18). The words we use and the way we treat others portray who we really are inside.

Our words reflect what's in our hearts, but our spoken words can also influence our hearts. This means we must guard our words so we can guard our hearts and guard our hearts so we can guard our words.

Proverbs 15:1

¹ A soft answer turns away wrath,
But a harsh word stirs up anger.

Proverbs 12:18

[18] *There is one who speaks like the piercings of a sword,*
But the tongue of the wise promotes health.

The words we speak are so powerful that James, Jesus's brother, committed the first twelve verses of the third chapter of his book solely to this topic. He compares the tongue to a ship's rudder and a horse's bridle, able to control the whole body. He also compares it to a forest fire that destroys everything in its path. However, the opposite is true also. The tongue not only produces negative effects but can also produce positive effects. Carefully spoken words can promote peace, calmness, and healing. Yes, God's word says positive words can promote physical healing!

Proverbs 29:11

[11] *A fool vents all his feelings,*
But a wise man holds them back.

Proverbs 17:27–28

[27] *He who has knowledge spares his words,*
And a man of understanding is of a calm spirit.
[28] *Even a fool is counted wise when he holds his peace;*
When he shuts his lips, he is considered perceptive.

Not everything needs to be repeated, and some things don't need to be said. We are not to speak simply because we know something or have something to say. The Holy Spirit will guide us before we speak if we first ask Him for support and guidance. If we can control what we say, can be trusted with a secret, and can avoid speaking out of anger, we will have favor and be considered wise and trustworthy. Even fools are considered to have some depth to their understanding when they simply keep their mouths shut and say nothing.

God's Word in Action

Look up the following verses in Proverbs to find the truth about the benefits and damages our words can cause.

Proverbs 10:19-20, 13:2-3, 16:24, 17:9, 18:6-8, 21:23, 26:20-23, and 29:8

Friendship

Proverbs 27:5–6

[5] Open rebuke is better
Than love carefully concealed.
[6] Faithful are the wounds of a friend,
But the kisses of an enemy are deceitful.

A true friend will tell us how it is, even if it is hurtful to hear it. Sometimes we will be tempted to consider it as cruel or given with ill-intent, but if this person is a friend, then that is likely not the case. Real friends will tell us things that others will not because they love us. Think twice before ending a friendship because a friend told you something that was difficult to hear. It was likely difficult for them to say it. Pride and anger often come forward and guide our actions in these situations if we aren't careful to guard our hearts.

We often don't see or can deny our shortcomings or the dangers that surround us. The people around us, who are uninfluenced by our emotions and commitments, can see our situation more objectively. We should always consider a friend's counsel, even if it hurts, although we should not accept their counsel without ample thought. It is also a good idea to follow up with a parent or other trusted adult when we receive difficult advice.

It takes courage to guard a friend from hurt or warn them about danger. Friendship works both ways. We may not want to confront a friend about something because we know it may hurt, but the word of God says, "faithful are the wounds of a friend."

A similar sentiment is expressed in Leviticus 19:17:

> [17]*"You shall not hate your brother in your heart. You shall surely rebuke your neighbor, and not bear sin because of him."*

And again, in Ezekiel 3:17–18:

> [17]*"Son of man, I have made you a watchman for the house of Israel; therefore hear a word from My mouth, and give them warning from Me:* [18]*When I say to the wicked, 'You shall surely die,' and you give him no warning, nor speak to warn the wicked from his wicked way, to save his life, that same wicked man shall die in his iniquity; but his blood I will require at your hand."*

In both passages we are told it is our Christian duty to tell a brother or a sister (meaning a fellow believer) if they are in sin, and to not disregard their sin for the sake of peace, favor, or gain.

Proverbs 12:26

[26]*The righteous should choose his friends carefully,*
For the way of the wicked leads them astray.

Proverbs 22:24–25

²⁴ Make no friendship with an angry man,
And with a furious man do not go,
²⁵ Lest you learn his ways
And set a snare for your soul.

True friendship is not something we offer lightly, and we may need to walk away from some friendships. When our friend has proven distrustful, dangerous, or jealous, it is okay to part ways. It is impossible to be friends with everyone, and it is impossible to please everyone.

God's Word in Action

Read this chapter with one of your friends, then talk about how what it says relates to your relationship. You can do this with more than one friend.

Equality

Proverbs 22:2

² The rich and the poor have this in common,
The LORD is the maker of them all.

In God's eyes we are all His children. Just as our parents love each child equally, God loves all His children equally. However, this does not mean we will all be equal in what we possess, or what we know, or what we accomplish in this life. This is also a reality in heaven. The Bible tells us that while we are not saved by works, we will be rewarded in heaven for our works done in faith and love. Not everyone will receive the same reward.

Matthew 16:27

²⁷ For the Son of Man will come in the glory of His
Father with His angels, and then He will reward each
according to his works.

Therefore, we will not all have the same material possessions in this life nor the same rewards in heaven, but we know God loves us all equally. That is our call as well; we must love all people equally, no matter if they are saved or lost, rich or poor, clean or dirty, educated or uneducated. When we love people equally, we are imitating Jesus and loving others as He did.

Luke 6:35–36

35 But love your enemies, do good, and lend, hoping for nothing in return; and your reward will be great, and you will be sons of the Most High. For He is kind to the unthankful and evil. 36 Therefore be merciful, just as your Father also is merciful.

Deuteronomy 15:11

11 For the poor will never cease from the land; therefore I command you, saying, 'You shall open your hand wide to your brother, to your poor and your needy, in your land.'

When we talk about equality, we are not saying everyone will have the same experiences in this life. That is impossible when we have free will because we are all free to make choices, and choices produce results, some of which will be positive and some negative. It is important that we all have equal access to opportunity, we all are treated with respect and dignity, and we all are free from the oppression of racism, while realizing our outcomes will differ. The world is not static; our world is highly variable and constantly changing. So much can be taken from us in the blink of an eye. As Christians we depend on God first to meet our needs and not the systems of this world. Often, He meets those needs through our brothers and sisters in the body of Christ, or the church.

Proverbs 29:13

13 The poor man and the oppressor have this in common: The LORD gives light to the eyes of both.

What matters the most is to realize that God created us all and He loves us all the same. This will allow us to love others as we love ourselves, the second greatest commandment given by Jesus Christ (see Leviticus 19:18). Of course, the first and greatest commandment is to love God with all your heart, soul, and strength (see Deuteronomy 6:5).

God's Word in Action

Look up the greatest commandment given by Jesus in Matthew 22:37-40 and compare it to what is written in Leviticus 19:18 and Deuteronomy 6:5.

Forward Thinking

Proverbs 24:27

²⁷ Prepare your outside work,
Make it fit for yourself in the field;
And afterward build your house.

Forward, or future, thinking is the ability to look ahead and determine what is needed to increase efficiency or to complete a project. It allows us to weigh the potential for success or failure and to act on it. Thinking this way makes us proactive, but it may involve risk. Is risk bad? Is it dangerous?

Proverbs 14:4

⁴ Where no oxen are, the trough is clean;
But much increase comes by the strength of an ox.

Why is buying an ox a risk? How does it apply to forward thinking? Without an ox the farmer doesn't have to spend any money to buy the ox, to buy grain for the ox, or do any work to prepare for the arrival and boarding of the ox. Like the proverb says, the feeding trough will only need cleaning if there is an ox to use it. The same efforts and resources to buy and care for the ox could have been spent elsewhere, or saved, or used for a vacation. These are decisions the farmer has to make, and any decision naturally assumes risk.

When we use our resources of time, energy, and money for something we don't have and is not critical for our survival, then we are taking risk to obtain it. It is risky for several reasons. The ox could die the next day and the farmer would lose the money and time invested. Or the farmer may become too busy with former commitments and never get around to using the ox, meaning the money and time spent on the ox was wasted. Or maybe the farmer bought the wrong kind of ox because he didn't know what he was doing, and then he had to go through the trouble of selling it and buying the correct one. The poor farmer spent more money and too much time to accomplish the same result.

Is risk worth it, even if we fail? Taking on risk will build character, teach life-changing lessons, and potentially increase personal position.

When we are considering a risky decision, we may encounter resistance and negativity from other people. Why? Sometimes they are genuinely concerned for us and the outcome. Other times they do not want to see us succeed; they might be envious of our potential. Maybe most often, those around us simply don't understand. They can't see what we see. They can't envision the potential benefits of a future move.

Risky decisions must always be thought out thoroughly to determine the potential for success. We must weigh the costs of the risk against the potential benefits. What does the farmer gain? Buying an ox, while it will require an additional chore (cleaning the trough), will help him accomplish more work, increase the amount of goods he can take to market, and will also be useful with other chores around the house or farm. The farmer that bought the ox was a forward thinker.

By using what God has already blessed us with, planning ahead, and taking on reasonable risk, we can realize an increase. An increase for a believer is an increase for the kingdom.

God's Word in Action

What are some of the risks and rewards associated with creating a candy bar fundraiser for your favorite charity? You will be in charge of the fundraiser from start to finish, from buying the candy bars to collecting the money and giving it to the charity.

Pretend you have a lawn care business. What are the risks and rewards of handing out gospel tracts to your customers?

Counsel

Proverbs 19:20, 27

²⁰ Listen to counsel and receive instruction,
That you may be wise in your latter days.

²⁷ Cease listening to instruction, my son,
And you will stray from the words of knowledge.

Receiving counsel from people means getting advice and guidance from those we can trust and those who have more experience than we have. Life experience comes with age and active living, and direct experience comes with involvement in the specific matter we are seeking advice on. Both types of experience can provide valuable insight when facing a problem.

It is crucial that we do not shy away from seeking help. Many people struggle with this and have suffered failures, repeated efforts, and burn-out as a result. When we ask for advice from those with experience, we save ourselves from unnecessary suffering, expense, wasted effort, and failure.

Proverbs 14:28

²⁸ *In a multitude of people is a king's honor,*
But in the lack of people is the downfall of a prince.

Proverbs 11:14

[14] Where there is no counsel, the people fall;
But in the multitude of counselors there is safety.

Pride keeps us from seeking counsel from others. We think that if we can do it alone then we will have all the reward, owing nothing to anyone else. Proverbs 14 tells us that the most powerful and successful people, like kings and princes, depend on a *multitude* of counselors to stay in power. Why would less be expected of us? People can help us in our endeavors. Sometimes people who may not be close to us are happy to give advice and counsel. Don't be afraid to ask. By asking for help and advice, we are also allowing God, your Father, to show us favor by putting people in our path who can help.

Proverbs 18:1

[1] A man who isolates himself seeks his own desire;
He rages against all wise judgment.

Proverbs 12:1

[1] Whoever loves instruction loves knowledge,
But he who hates correction is stupid.

Proverbs 18:1 warns us against this going-it-alone attitude. It is a type of isolation. It says when we do this, we seek our own desire. If we are seeking our own desire, then we are serving self and we have rejected God, refusing to serve Him and only Him. This is a deep and difficult teaching, but the word of

God tells us it is truth. Proverbs 12:1 adds to this idea and says a person who hates counsel is *stupid.* Clearly, if God is comparing counsel to wisdom and knowledge, then it is a godly and righteous thing to seek. If we can avoid costly mistakes and wasting precious time, then we are being better stewards of the resources God has blessed us with and can give more back to the kingdom of God.

<u>God's Word in Action</u>

Re-read Proverbs 12:1. Put in your own words what a person who loves instruction gains and what a person who hates correction loses.

Leadership

Proverbs 16:10–15

¹⁰ Divination is on the lips of the king;
His mouth must not transgress in judgment.
¹¹ Honest weights and scales are the LORD's;
All the weights in the bag are His work.
¹² It is an abomination for kings to commit wickedness,
For a throne is established by righteousness.
¹³ Righteous lips are the delight of kings,
And they love him who speaks what is right.
¹⁴ As messengers of death is the king's wrath,
But a wise man will appease it.
¹⁵ In the light of the king's face *is* life,
And his favor is like a cloud of the latter rain.

The Bible is clear that a position of leadership is not to be taken lightly. A leader must not be dishonest, even though the temptation to be dishonest will often surface. He must not commit wickedness, and he must always be righteous. He must speak what is right, never lying or speaking in unjust anger. The leader must be able to judge his subjects courageously and righteously. Finally, the people respectfully fear the leader, and likewise they enjoy being in his favor. The spirit of discernment must be strong in a leader.

Guided by Wisdom

Being a leader is not an easy task, and it is not for everyone. Difficult decisions must be made, decisions that often require give and take, or negotiation, wise discernment, and dependable counsel. Becoming a leader, whether it is in business, politics, or a neighborhood Bible study, is in essence becoming a public representative of God. The Bible says in Romans 13 that God puts leaders into their positions, and in passages like Proverbs 16:10–15, He gives the guidelines on how they are to perform.

Romans 13:1–3

[1] Let every soul be subject to the governing authorities. For there is no authority except from God, and the authorities that exist are appointed by God. [2] Therefore whoever resists the authority resists the ordinance of God, and those who resist will bring judgment on themselves. [3] For rulers are not a terror to good works, but to evil. Do you want to be unafraid of the authority? Do what is good, and you will have praise from the same.

Being a leader requires having "tough skin" and a "strong backbone." These terms are used because leaders are often attacked by the very people they love and serve. They must also judge and punish, or reward, those same people. It is impossible to please everyone and there will always be someone who does not like the leader. A leader must anticipate this response to his or her presence and decisions and must be able to respond with grace, when required, and with stern action, when required.

Our world is a hectic and sometimes scary place, and the reason often lies on the shoulders of an unjust leader, who desires to hold onto power or gain more power at the expense of others. They have their reward in full on this side of heaven, meaning they have forfeited their heavenly reward. As leaders appointed by God, they have turned their backs on Him and have done things their way. This is why leaders, more than most, should be on their knees begging God for wisdom and guidance, favor and strength, always praying without ceasing.

We to, must constantly pray for our leaders. They have much responsibility and pressure. They are responsible for many lives, and they are in constant bombardment of temptation and persuasion. If you find yourselves in a leadership position, lead with God, lead with courage, and lead with honesty.

God's Word in Action

Look up 1 Timothy 2:1-2 and choose three leaders you can pray for. Choose one from the national level, like a president or a senator. Choose one from your community, like a small business owner or the mayor. Finally, pray for your parents.

Freedom

Proverbs 5:21–22

21 For the ways of man are before the eyes of the LORD,
And He ponders all his paths.
22 His own iniquities entrap the wicked man,
And he is caught in the cords of his sin.

What is freedom? At a national level, it means that our country is not ruled by any other country. On an individual level, it can mean that we are not controlled by anyone or anything. It may also mean that we are able to act, think, or speak in any manner we please. The Bible compares sinful behavior with being bound in chains or being enslaved. What is sinful behavior? It is doing what we want apart from God. In contrast, God says following His law and doing what He says is freedom.

We all serve somebody. All of us. Either we choose to serve God, or we choose to serve Satan. Choosing not to serve God is the same as choosing to serve Satan. This is what Jesus meant when He said, "If you're not with Me, you're against Me" (see Matthew 12:30).

Proverbs 21:1

¹ The king's heart is in the hand of the LORD,
Like the rivers of water;
He turns it wherever He wishes.

Whether we like it or not, or if we acknowledge it or not, this world and our lives are standing on a spiritual component that is more powerful and more significant than the physical component we all live in and experience every day. That spiritual component is controlled by God, which means He also has the means to ensure His will, or His plan, shall come to pass, regardless of our stubborn and disobedient hearts, or what we do or don't do. Proverbs 21:1 tells us God holds the hearts of the most powerful men in His hands, and He directs them where He pleases.

This should be encouraging to us. God is showing us that if we leave Him and go our own way, we have not realized freedom from Him. He is still present, and He is still in control. This should strengthen our commitment to God and validate that true freedom is found when we serve the living God!

Psalm 119:44–45

⁴⁴ So shall I keep Your law continually,
Forever and ever.
⁴⁵ And I will walk at liberty,
For I seek Your precepts.

Some people think they would not be free to do what they wanted to do if they believed in God and followed Him. They claim God's rules are out of touch with the human experience and take all the fun out of life.

We need to ask ourselves this question: Why would God create us and this world, only to remove true enjoyment from it? The answer is He would not do that. True enjoyment of this life is found through and with God.

The way of God offers freedom, peace, and wisdom, without sacrificing fun. Not following the way of God brings the opposite. If we refuse God because we don't want to be controlled or to miss out on fun, what we are really doing is refusing to let go of our sin. This "fun" usually looks like getting drunk, using drugs, dating multiple people, hoarding money, seeking popularity and fame, gossiping, and the list goes on. All these things come with problems; they come with chains. What appears in the beginning to be freedom turns into bondage through addiction, feelings of inadequacy and loss, debt, greed, bitterness, envy, and trashed relationships.

Walking with God offers a more fulfilling life. God offers true freedom. He offers you eternal salvation, knowledge, and wisdom this world cannot understand; he gives us a peace no one can explain; he gives us His Holy Spirit and His love. These things set us free, and this freedom is found when we humbly choose to serve and love God with all our heart, soul, and mind.

Matthew 6:33–34

"33 But seek first the kingdom of God and His righteousness, and all these things shall be added to you. 34 Therefore do not worry about tomorrow, for tomorrow will worry about its own things. Sufficient for the day is its own trouble."

Jesus promised to give us everything we needed if we would put Him first. This allows us to live a life free from worry!

God's Word in Action

Look up the words of Apostle Paul in 1 Corinthians 6:12. In your own words, write what this verse means and give an example of something you are able to do but choose not to do because it is not good, or helpful.

Envy and Contentment

Proverbs 24:19–20

¹⁹ Do not fret because of evildoers,
Nor be envious of the wicked;
²⁰ For there will be no prospect for the evil man;
The lamp of the wicked will be put out.

Envy is when we want something that someone else has. It can also cause us to resent the person who has what we want and desire that they lose what they have so we feel better about ourselves. Envy is also called covetousness; it is the focus of the tenth commandment.

Exodus 20:17

¹⁷ "You shall not covet your neighbor's house; you shall not covet your neighbor's wife, nor his male servant, nor his female servant, nor his ox, nor his donkey, nor anything that is your neighbor's."

Being envious of what another person has and desiring to get it is covetousness. It was this commandment that convicted the apostle Paul of his sin nature. Before he met Jesus and was saved, when the veil, or in his case, scales (see Acts 9:18), was lifted from his eyes, he saw the sin of covetousness in his life, and he was convicted. He now knew he wasn't perfect, and the foundation he stood on crumbled beneath him. He knew he wasn't worthy of standing before the God he served so faithfully, and he knew he needed a savior. That Savior is Jesus Christ.

Proverbs 14:30

30 A sound heart is life to the body,
But envy is rottenness to the bones.

The opposite of envy is contentment. Envy is like rottenness to our bones, which means it steals the joy of life from us. Contentment is peace. When we are content with what the Lord has blessed us with, and we know we have worked hard and well, we have been honest and not gained illicitly, then we have peace in our surroundings. Imagine two identical families in which the only difference is one has a lot and the other has a little. With God in the hearts of both families, the family who has less will be just as joyful as the family with more. If the family with more does not have God in their hearts, then they will look to their belongings to bring them joy, and they will not find it. Likewise, if the family with less rejects God in their house, then they may turn to bitterness and blame for their lack. The heart that has God has His favor. We need nothing more than that, to keep God in our hearts. He will take care of us.

The family who is blessed with abundance must guard their hearts from envy all the more, for riches only lead to a desire for more riches. The lust for money and possession is insatiable, there is never an adequate amount to attain. If we are blessed, we must not forget from where, or from whom, our blessings came, and always be generous with what we have. Give back to

God by giving to His kingdom and to the needy among us, because all that we have has been given to us by God and belongs to Him.

God's Word in Action

Think of something that you don't have but really want. Maybe a video game, new clothes, or a new bike. Now consider the things God has blessed you with already, like your old bike and your current wardrobe. Practice being content with what you have today.

Diligence and Laziness

Proverbs 10:4–5

⁴ He who has a slack hand becomes poor,
But the hand of the diligent makes rich.
⁵ He who gathers in summer is a wise son;
He who sleeps in harvest is a son who causes shame.

Few things in life will earn more favor and respect and increase the prospects of success and blessing than diligence. Diligence means we work carefully and persistently. Careful work means we are intentional at doing it right and doing it well. Persistent work means we do not give up when it gets hard and we finish the job, every time, when it is in our power to do so. Sometimes it will not be easy to finish what we start, and we'll want to give up. A person of strong character will work hard, sacrifice, and use creative thinking to complete a job. A diligent person does not quit.

Proverbs 27:23–26

²³ Be diligent to know the state of your flocks,
And attend to your herds;
²⁴ For riches are not forever,
Nor does a crown endure to all generations.
²⁵ When the hay is removed, and the tender grass shows

101

itself,
And the herbs of the mountains are gathered in,
[26] *The lambs will provide your clothing,*
And the goats the price of a field.

We are all called to provide for ourselves, not to depend on an inheritance or the efforts of others to sustain us. Likewise, we must be carefully and persistently diligent to know what is happening around us as it relates to our work and our livelihoods. We must know the condition of our products, tools, equipment, and coworkers. Never assume *anything*, always being diligent to stay informed, without stepping outside of our authority. When we take care of the smaller details, our preparations and efforts will begin to provide for us. The diligent worker is one who cares about the details, and our superiors will notice that.

Proverbs 21:25–26

[25] *The desire of the lazy man kills him,*
For his hands refuse to labor.
[26] *He covets greedily all day long,*
But the righteous gives and does not spare.

The rewards for hard work and determination are far more reaching than the immediate rewards of food, clothing, shelter, and money. When a follower of Christ achieves success through hard work, the kingdom of God is blessed. When we are lazy, we are acting outside of God's will for our lives. Why? Because laziness restricts our ability to bless others who are in need and inhibits us from doing the work God has for us. This relates to Proverbs 21:25 where it plainly tells us the desire of a lazy man kills him. It is spiritual death, and we know that because God tells us in verse 26 that the righteous give and do not spare. They are doing the work of God, and since they are contrasted with a lazy person, we know diligence and hard work are righteous traits. It is good news to know that when we work hard we will be rewarded spiritually as well as physically.

Proverbs 21:5

5 The plans of the diligent lead surely to plenty,
But those of everyone who is hasty, surely to poverty.

Beware of anything that promises quick and easy results. There is nothing quick in life that will sustain us. Everything we have must be earned by not only hard work but also by work done correctly and in excellence. It took over ten years to build our family-owned business into a sustainable company that provided *plenty* for our family. In those ten years our family had very little money, we suffered through ups and downs, we were on welfare for a short time, and we learned how to be careful in how we used our money. As a result of this persistent effort and careful spending our company has seen periods where it has operated debt free. This has allowed us to bless the kingdom of God by blessing others in His name.

Proverbs 6:10–11

10 A little sleep, a little slumber,
A little folding of the hands to sleep—
11 So shall your poverty come on you like a prowler,
And your need like an armed man.

Resting and taking breaks are acceptable and reasonable and are not signs of laziness. What we need to be aware of is the development of bad habits. A little of this and a little of that, can soon develop into a lifestyle. Diligence means we work even when we don't feel like it. Laziness means we don't work if we don't feel like it. Work must be part of our lifestyle and character, otherwise our needs will *come on us like an armed man,* meaning they will control us. If we have a need but do not have the means, then we can be controlled by the provider of those needs. Be it the government, an institution, a criminal, or even a saint, we don't want to be under the power of another because we can't provide for ourselves. These are the results of the evils of debt.

A little sleep and a little slumber can have spiritual consequences too. If we slack off in our time spent with God, we can experience a gradual spiritual decline. Be persistent and committed in meeting with God every day, for this is part of His will for everyone.

God's Word in Action

The next time someone asks you for help, stick around after the job is done and help clean up tools or trash at the worksite. This is diligence in action and is good practice for the future.

Revenge and Justice

Proverbs 20:22

²² Do not say, "I will recompense evil";
Wait for the LORD, and He will save you.

Revenge is in direct opposition to love, which is God's most precious commandment. When we desire revenge, we desire for someone else to be damaged or hurt in some way. We also are acting selfishly, wanting to receive what we feel is due to us. When we desire revenge, we do not believe God is in control and we are not walking in faith. We are becoming the judge.

The desire for revenge also allows anger to grow. At its root, revenge is unforgiveness with an added desire to act on it. It fuels bitterness and hate, feelings which may not have existed if it were not for the always-present desire to see revenge come to pass.

While revenge appears to be a natural reaction to a legitimate wrong committed against another, it is not. Revenge is like an evil impostor, pretending to be something else—justice.

Deuteronomy 19:15

¹⁵ *"One witness shall not rise against a man concerning any iniquity or any sin that he commits; by the mouth of two or three witnesses the matter shall be established.*

105

Guided by Wisdom

Whenever a wrong, or an injustice, is committed against someone, we want justice to prevail. Justice is never enacted on a personal level; it is enacted on a communal level. The Bible says there must be two or three witnesses to judge a man. Our justice system requires a person to appear before a court to be tried by his or her peers. Guilt or innocence is never determined by a single person.

Proverbs 31:8–9

[8] Open your mouth for the speechless,
In the cause of all who are appointed to die.
[9] Open your mouth, judge righteously,
And plead the cause of the poor and needy.

When we see wrongs committed against the poor, the speechless, and the needy and we come to their defense, we are participating in God's biblical standards of justice. We become the second witness alongside the first witness, who is the victim. This fulfills the requirements of Deuteronomy 19:15. The need for revenge can be extinguished when courageous and proactive men and women of God stand up for justice on one another's behalf. It is the duty of the believer to speak out against injustices being committed against those who cannot defend themselves.

Psalm 56:8

[8] You number my wanderings;
Put my tears into Your bottle;
Are they not in Your book?

How do we free ourselves from this seemingly natural desire to see personal justice served when we have no communal path to accomplish it? For example, if someone steals a candy bar on the bus and eats it, but nobody else saw it, then there is not a second or third witness, or a court system to enact justice. In this case we may not be able to get help and the justice we deserve. Proverbs 20:22 frees us from the burden of seeking revenge by telling us that God has our back. There is no injustice He does not see, no injustice against one of His children He does not record. In fact, every tear shed by one of His children resulting from an injustice is collected by God and stored in His bottle. God is for us, He loves us, and He is the most powerful, most awesome Spirit in existence. When someone wrongs us, and we have no way of getting justice outside of seeking our own revenge, we must lift it up to God.

God's Word in Action

Justice, revenge, and simply letting things go can be hard topics to navigate at your age. Read Romans 12:17-21, with verse 19 as your focus. Let these verses give you faith that God is always with you and for you. You never have to do it alone.

Psalm 78:4

⁴ We will not hide them from their children, telling to the generation to come the praises of the LORD, And His strength and His wonderful works that He has done.

Afterward

By reading this book you have familiarized yourself with the truth of God's word. I encourage you to continue reading the Bible, and to read the gospel accounts of Jesus Christ in the books of Matthew, Mark, Luke, and John. In the Gospel's you will find the fulfillment of the Old Testament prophecies and the salvation provided to us through Jesus Christ.

You can give your life to Jesus today. It doesn't matter how old, or how young, you are. Jesus said in Matthew 19 and Luke 18, "Let the little children come to Me, and do not forbid them; for of such is the kingdom of heaven." If you feel in your heart today that you are ready to give your life to Jesus, then you simply tell Him. Tell Him you want to live your life with Him as your Lord and King, and you want to serve Him in all you do. Tell Him you love Him, and you desire to be guided and taught by the Holy Spirit. Tell Him you believe He is the Son of God and what the Bible says about Him is true, that He died for your sins, He rose again three days later, and He now sits at the right hand of God, the Father. After you do that, tell your parents and your pastor you accepted Jesus Christ as your Lord and Savior so they can pray for you and help you as you walk this path.

About the Author

Chris Long is a son of God, saved and loved by Jesus, and is blessed with the Holy Spirit. He is married to his best-friend, Caroll Buitrago-Long, and they have two children, Daniela and David.

He writes many forms of prose, including song lyrics, blogs, Christian nonfiction, short-story fiction, and fiction novels.

He has recorded two albums, *The Tragedy of Complexity* (2020), and *By His Name* (2023). Physical copies can be purchased at https://singwriteread.com/music/, or downloaded from any streaming platform.

His blog, which focuses on the walk of the believer, can be found at https://singwriteread.com/the-blog/.

Chris's books can be purchased on his website https://singwriteread.com/books/ or on Amazon.com.

Sign up for Chris's newsletter at Sing Write Read to stay up to date on new music and book releases, concert dates, and book signings. And please come along with us on social media. Subscribe, follow, like, share, and comment. We love to hear from you.

Guided by Wisdom

Contact Chris anytime to place custom or bulk orders of his products via email or his website at:

chrislong.swr@gmail.com

https://singwriteread.com/

Follow Chris on social media at:

https://www.youtube.com/@chrislong1046

https://www.facebook.com/ChrisLong.SWR/

https://www.instagram.com/SingWriteRead/

https://chrislong-swr.bandcamp.com/releases

Made in the USA
Monee, IL
27 October 2024

68119410R00075